Interior Design Series

HOTEL KALEIDOSCOPE

LIAONING SCIENCE AND TECHNOLOGY PUBLISHING HOUSE

Publisher: Liaoning Science and Technology Publishing House

　　　　　　NO.25, 11Wei Road, Heping District, Shenyang, 110003

Printer: SNP Leefeng

Distributor: Pace Publishing Limited

Size: 240mm×280mm

Word: 50,000

Print run: 1 ～ 1700 copies

Publishing: 2007.11

Printing: 2007.11

Editor: Chen Chiliang

Cover Design: Li Ying

Layout Design: Li Ying

Proof Reading: Zhong Shumin

ISBN 978-7-5381-5184-8

Contact: 86-24-23284360

Email: lkzzb@mail.lnpgc.com.cn

Web: www.lnkj.com.cn

Foreword

With the booming in fashion and tourism, there come the creative class who adore fashion, court design and enjoy life. Normally the starred hotels are too commercialized, where service style is too invariable and standardized. Therefore they can't arouse the interest of the creative class. Whereas boutique hotels spare no efforts in their design so that they are nicknamed the "design hotels", which, out of sheer bored sensation towards the traditional hotels, turn out to be a betrayer to the traditional ones. As has been pointed out by the Polish poet Wislawa Szymborska, beautiful is such a certainty, but uncertainty is more beautiful. Here compiled in this book are unpredictably beautiful worlds for you to explore.

Brilliant boutique hotels in Germany, Britain, America, Italy, Austria, Spain, China and so on are selected in this book. High resolution pictures will demonstrate the unique design concept from different angles, with detailed exposition for every creative aspect. Anyway, boutique hotels are still hotels that belong to the service industry, and therefore underneath every detail of the design is the concern to offer more considerate and humane service. In a word, it is a book that provides invaluable inspiration for hotel owners and interior designers and helpful reference for tourists.

Contents

Designer: Jestico + Whiles / Date: 2002 / Location: Prague, Czech Republic
Photographer: Ales Jungmann

Andel's Hotel

The guest first enters a cool, uncluttered lobby, the floor of warm limestone, contrasting with textured, roughly split stone to the core walls. In the centre, a full length translucent curtain defines the seating "rooms"

The reception desk is a heavy, monolithic block of honed stone, with inset writing blocks of stacked glass. All operational equipment is concealed within the desk. The restaurant seats over 200 guests in large groups or at intimate tables for four or two. The back wall is at panelled in stone as in the reception, but carved into this are two buffets lined in saturated coloured polished plaster. Angled mirrors on the back wall are used to evoke the traditional brasserie, and refcect the subtly glowing glass opposite. This zone can also be used for more formal dining experience.

In the bathrooms, the lavatory and shower are in separate enclosures, defined by frameless glass doors, through which a single wall of flame coloured glass glows, warming the whole room. An enamelled wash basin is set at perfect working height, raised above a low wash stand of dove grey marble, and in front of an illuminated, partially frosted mirror. The floor is of warm honey coloured limestone.

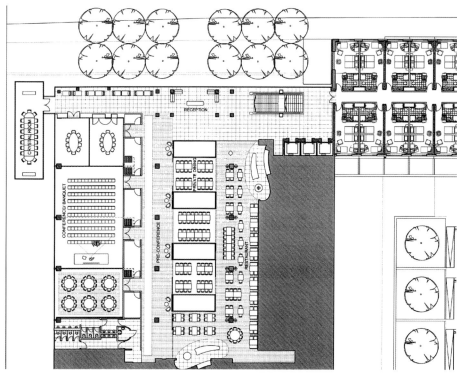

9

Designer: Tihany Design / Date: 2003 / Location: Rome, Italy
Photographer: Janos Grapow Andrea Martiradonna

Aleph Hotel

Tihany's ever-present wit is predominant throughout the hotel with his provocative interpretation of heaven and hell. Two full-scale samurai figures, representing the eternal dichotomy of "good versus evil," stand guard at the hotel's entrance and set the whimsical tone. "Hell" is represented by a saturated red interior on the ground floor in the Lobby Bar & Wine Lounge. The casual elegant "Sin" restaurant continues the metaphor with its red leather and velvet chairs, tinted red glass accents throughout, red glass and tableware, and even by serving an all-red menu.

Tihany's Library Lounge, with custom mahogany wood paneling, red leather upholstered furniture, and bookshelves lined with holographic "books," is sexy and sophisticated.In an unexpected design twist, "heaven," is downstairs on the cellar level. The pristine white Aleph Spa is complete with training facilities, steam room, sauna, and a pool inspired by Roman baths. Slip into a robe and melt into the specially designed relaxation lounge for a refreshing drink.Each guest room features a significant black and white photomural created expressly for the hotel by New York street photographer, Bram Tihany. Depicting special moments in "a day in the life of Rome," these poignant images portray a sense of place and infuse the rooms with energy. The combination of contemporary and period furnishings is true to living in modern Rome. The specially designed VIP suite, finished in exotic zebrawood, features a 76-square-meter private terrace and an enclosed Jacuzzi.

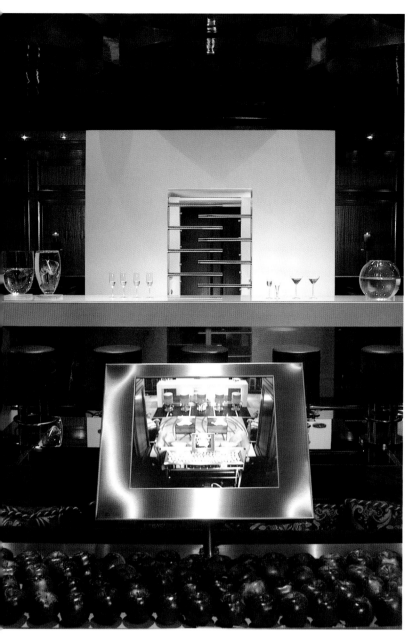

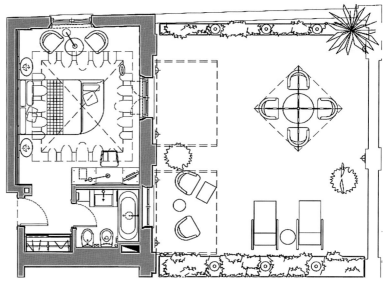

Designer: Rainer Seiferth / Date: 2003 / Location: Berlin, Germany
Photographer: Rainer Seiferth

Arte Luise Kunsthotel

In March, 2003, this section also celebrated a ceremonial opening officiated by the presiding government minister. The hotel comprised almost 50 rooms and a gallery for art. Künstlerheim Luise is like a true hotel. It is on the road to success as a "museum where you can spend the night". The current generation of artists is international and renowned. Each of them has made his or her room into a unique work of art: "rooms like dreams", as one large German daily paper recently cominented.

The concept of this somewhat different hotel – "art instead of grandeur, poetry instead of room service" – is winning guests over. A French film director, who immediately took a room for several weeks told the reception: "I know all the hotels in this world, believe me. And I hate them all. But I love your hotel. And Paris will learn of my love." Not only Paris.

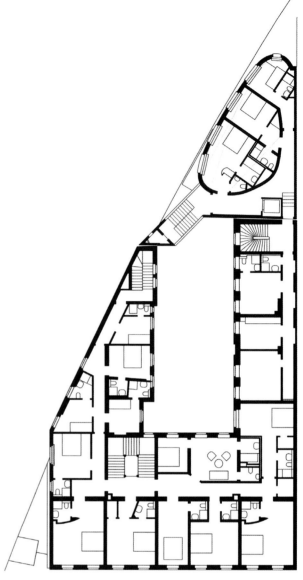

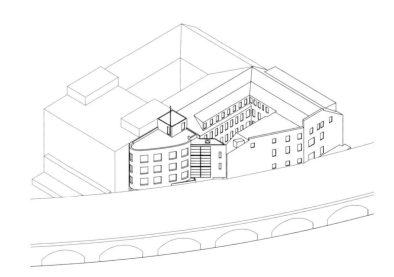

31

Designer: Tilla Teus / Date: 2004 / Location: Zurich, Switzerland / Photographer: A. Rindlisbacher

Bellerive au Lac

A major theme, featured throughout the building, is the surface detailing or interior linings from the foyer with its cool stone slabs to the conference room clad in warm cherry wood and the dining rooms with sumptuous leather and textiles, right up to the hotel bedrooms with oak and mirrors. The materials and impeccable craftsmanship create an agreeable, elegant ambience.

The abundance of daylight is a further asset. The open layout of the rooms facing the lake affords views from deep within the building. The conference and fitness areas are grouped around an atrium as a source of light. The light shaft, formalizing an outdoor space, now serves as an intimate, light-filled lounge.

Designer: Jan Kleihues, Kleihues + Kleihues / Date: 2005 / Location: Berlin, Germany
Photographer: Stefan Müller

Concorde Hotel

Hotel Conorde is a new buiding of the French hote groug Louvre Hotels. Jan Kleihues was asked to design both its exterior and interior. Being positioned right next to the renowned Kurfürstendamm the hotel includes 267 rooms, 44 suites, 8 seminar rooms, a ballroom, a restaurant, a bar and a wellness area.

The interior as well as the exterior of the hotel show one clear artistic vision. Its 17 storeys narrow to the corner and develop vertically with numerous setbacks. The interior was designed in a timeless deduced elegance being highly modern but independent from any fashion.

Numerous pieces such as armchairs, lamps, doorknobs and even carpets were exclusively designed for the hotel. Dominant materials are walnut timber, smoked oak timber, corean and Carrara marble.

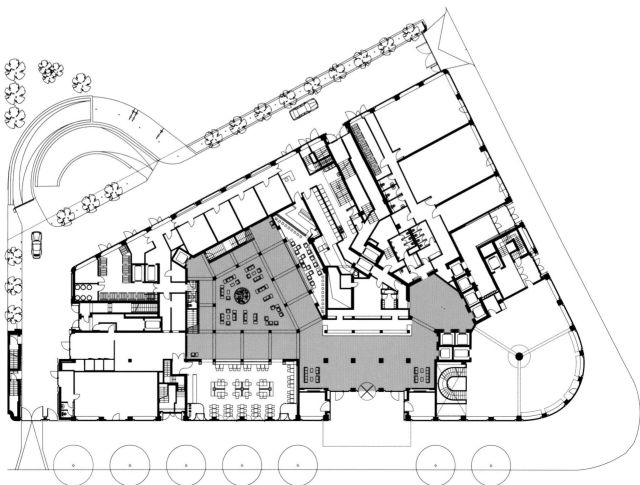

Designer: JOI-Design Innenarchitekten GmbH / Date: 2006 / Location: Cologne, Germany
Dom Hotel

The Dom Hotel is one of the oldest luxury hotels in Germany(with a history of more than 140 years), and it is a synonymous for traditional top hospitality. Due to its location close to the famous cathedral in Cologne it is an icon for hotels in Germany.

With the "Sir Peter Ustinov's Bar International" and the restaurant "Le Mérou", Dom Hotel now becomes anew to see and to be seen.

The majority of the new design elements are rather modern, although the colours reflect the ancient times, but over all the traditional architecture sets a strong frame, which ties the history with the present time.

A highlighted reception desk made of glass goes perfectly with the old marble columns, and the modern leather chairs in the restaurant stand for a distinguished freshness. The new "Sir Peter Ustinov's Bar International" now links the lobby with the restaurant and the winter garden making the hotel much more transparent and open than it was before.

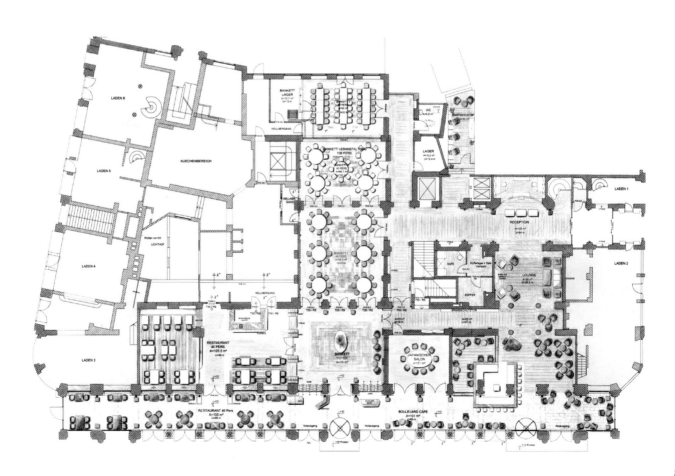

Designer: Werner Aisslinger / Date: 2005 / Location: Graz, Austria
Photographer: Studio Aisslinger

Daniel Hotel

In the centre of Graz, within a few minutes' walk from the historic town, the convention centre, and the Kunsthaus (House of Art), the Daniel, due to open in June 2005, will be a lively, fresh and artistic landmark on the map of the former European City of Culture. Designed by Berlin-based designer Werner Aisslinger, the hotel with its 101 stylishly furnished guestrooms bears his functional, yet highly intelligent and innovative signature. The result is both the warm and authentic touch of the region is captured whilst meeting the demands of the young and well-travelled culture aficionado.

With a large public area adaptable for events, an internet corner and a meeting room for up to 12, all business needs are easily taken care of at the Daniel. Appealing to guests that maintain a spontaneous lifestyle, the bar and restaurant area is cheerfully open plan, providing ample opportunity to mingle and interact with the local scene. While the breakfast terrace, the fireside lounge and the library cater amply for the more leisurely at heart, and the Espresso Bar with tapas counter offers guests a flexible range of modern cuisine.

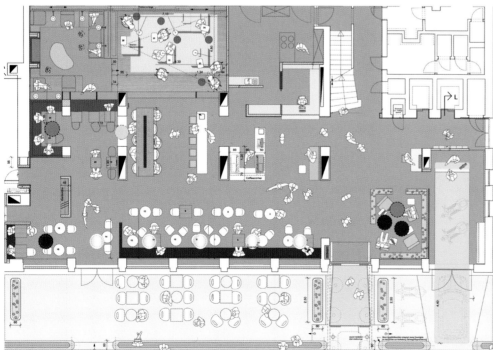

Designer: Bost Berlin – Interieur Design / Date: 2002 / Location: Weimar, Germany
Photographer: Andreas Muhs

Elephant Hotel

Apart from the public spaces at five-star Hotel Elephant in Weimar, Germany, Bost Berlin redesigned the bar and three suites.

The spacious lobby is highlighted by a handmade trilogy of high-grade steel luminaries. The back-lit modern-age reception sets another creative accent. Makassar wall boardings and illuminated circular pillars correspond harmoniously with the shiny marble flooring in the lobby.

Using contrasty colourings corresponding with pure and structured forms the designers created the interiors of "Marlene Bar" in Art Déco style. A cubic shape has been given to the bar with its illuminated marble surfaces. Interpreted contemporarily, the interior of the suites reflects the hotel's eventful history. Wall-mounted unique copies in the suites remind one of their famous name givers: Thomas Mann, Johannes Daniel Falk and Udo Lindenberg.

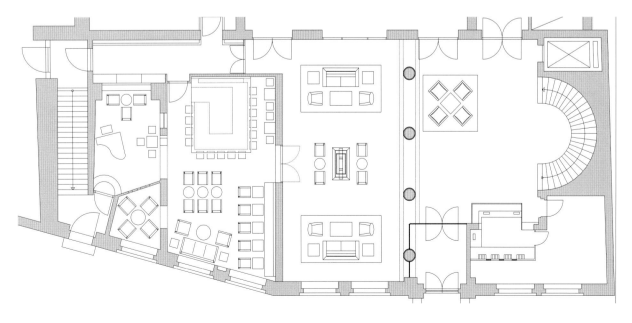

Designer: Carl Ross Design, Inc. / Date: 2005 / Location: Barbados
Photographer: Robert Miller Photography

Hilton Barbados

This new-construction hotel is the focal point of the Needham's Point peninsula, site of historic 17th century Fort Charles, St. Ann's Garrison, and one of Barbados' only remaining lighthouses. One of the project's main goals was to create a world-class destination resort infused with unmistakable local colour.

The dynamic Careenage Bar design is based on the historic port of Bridgetown where old sailing ships would be tipped over or "careened" to be reconditioned. Rich wood tones are blended with bright fabrics, exotic furniture styles and found objects. Nautical-theme accessories and artifacts are blended with historical rum production artifacts (rum was originally invented in Barbados) donated to the property by Mount Gay Distilleries Ltd., who has been producing rum in Barbados for over 300 years.

The Lighthouse Terrace offers a fresh, colorful, casual dining experience, richly patterned limestone floor, and one-of-a-kind mosaic tabletops overlooking the luscious landscaped pools and beaches below. The brightly coloured accent "flower wall" features fresh-daily, locally grown tropical flowers, and the hand stenciled, cove-lit ceilings borrow their patterning from the wooden trim work of the famous Barbadian "Chattel Houses" of days gone by.

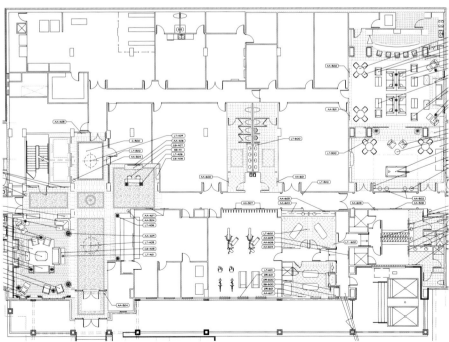

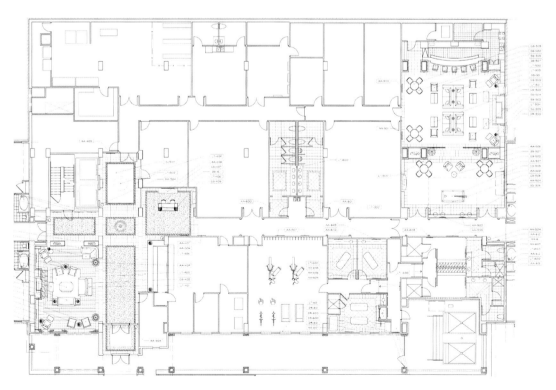

Designer: Jestico + Whiles / Date: 2006 / Location: London, UK / Photographer: James Morris
Hilton Canary Wharf

Hilton London Canary Wharf, as the name suggests, is at Canary Wharf, London Docklands. Jestico + Whiles was appointed as interior designer for this 14- floor, 286- room Hilton hotel, part of the Discovery Dock West development at South Quay.

The ground floor is a continuous space, comprising reception, lobby bar and restaurant, in which pools of light, rich highlights of colour and contrasting textures emphasize features and define zones.

The reception desk is a simple block of honed stone, and the bar is of lucent pond green glass and the staircase is encased in shimmering mesh. A rough wall of moss and rust coloured riven slate runs the full length of the space, studded with glowing panels of deep green glass, carved away in places to enclose suede–lined slugs and niches.

The bedrooms are designed with equal measures of style, function and comfort, with bathrooms in warm stone finishes and splashes of coloured glass. An executive sky lounge has stunning views down the Thames to St Paul's Cathedral.

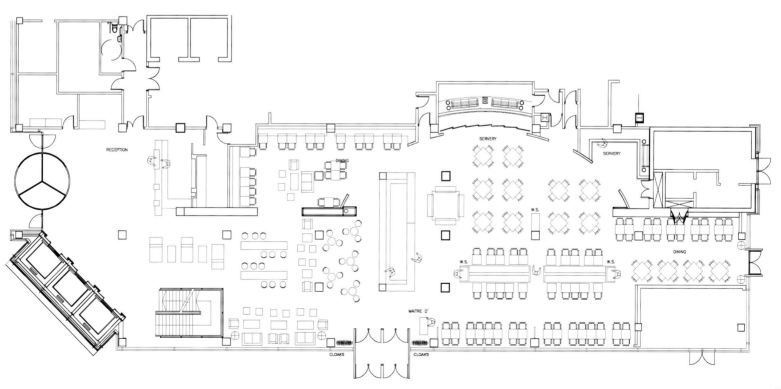

Designer: Jestico + Whiles / Date: 2005 / Location: Belfast, UK / Photographer: James Morris

Malmaison Belfast Hotel

Like many of the Malmaison hotels, the existing building Malmaison Belfast contributes much to its character. But it is the way the designers selectively retain elements of the existing fabric and combine them with new furniture, fittings and finishes that produces the full effect. Here, the original vast arched windows, ornate iron columns and deep timber beams dominate the bar and brasserie but are softened by subtle lighting, rich colours and sensuous textures. In some bedrooms, the sloping ceilings and wooden beams generate a cozy impression, which is complemented by velvety or silken fabrics.

Malmaison Belfast builds on Jestico + Whiles's extensive portfolio of design for the hotelier. Again, the familiar theme of expressing the brand's association with Parisian fun, flamboyance and luxury, while reflecting the hotel's specific location, is employed. Artistic photographs depict Belfast's nearby historic port. Details, such as an internal window that is a contemporary take on Art Nouveau, evoke Paris; and the stone period building, which is transformed by dramatic new lighting, would not look out of place in the City of Romance.

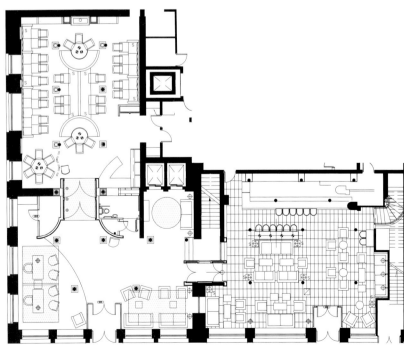

Designer: Fabiola Zeka Lorenzi / Date: 2003 / Location: Padova, Italy
Photographer: Paolo Poli, Fabiola Zeka Lorenzi

Methis Hotel

Methis means "mixture", to emphasize the universal meaning of the four elements in all the different cultures worldwide; furthermore the word "mixture" reminds us of the four elements– air, earth, fire and water– coming together in the interiors of every floor.

The old building of the 1950s has acquired a new identity thanks to a precise chromatic choice.The white colour of the facade introduces and anticipates the game of colours of the interiors,emphasizing character, meaning and function of the room.

Every element can be chromatically identified in the furnishing and finishing touches of the four floors: warm shades from ivory to brown to evoke earth, the seduction of red to suggest fire, the light nuances of blue and azure to indicate water, and the transparency of white and silver to imply air in the fourth floor, where panoramic suites with exclusive terraces are located.

59 rooms are distributed on the four floors, each made differently according to which one of the four elements is the main theme.In each room, there is one furnishing ornament, an ethnic object that refers to the main theme, the only eccentric aspect in this rigorous minimalism.

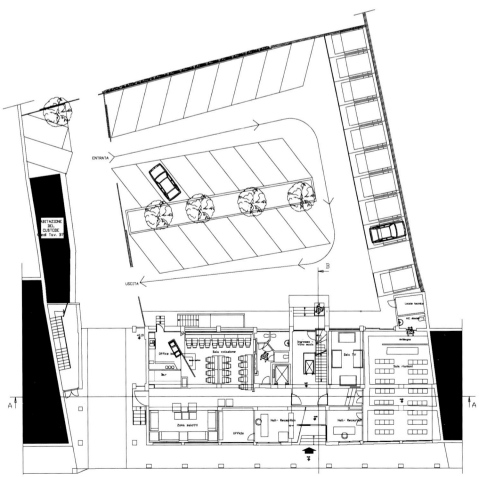

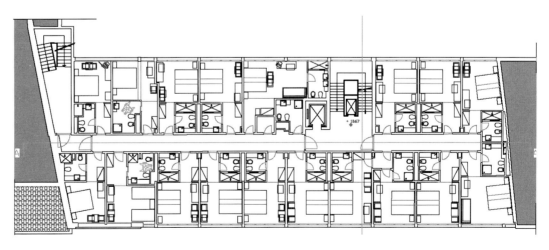

Designer: Pia M. Schmid & Karsten Schmidt / Date: 2004 / Location: Berlin, Germany
Photographer: Andrea Flak

Mövenpick Hotel

The most important feature of this project is its pure individualism. The combination of innovative interior design and a firework display of colours, shapes and materials band together to create an entire work of art in Mövenpick Hotel Berlin, situated inside the historic and protected Siemens building.

Reflected everywhere is the play of the elements fire, water, air and light, giving a dynamic and yet subtle and sensitively transformed architecture within the historical walls.

An architectonic feature of the building is the four inner courtyards, which are connected to each other via a footbridge.

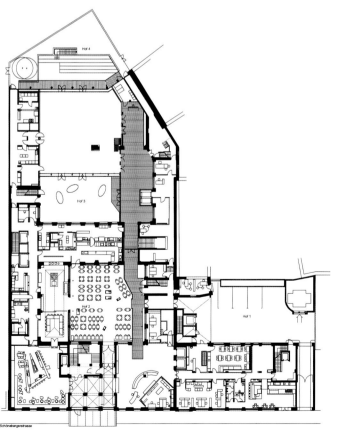

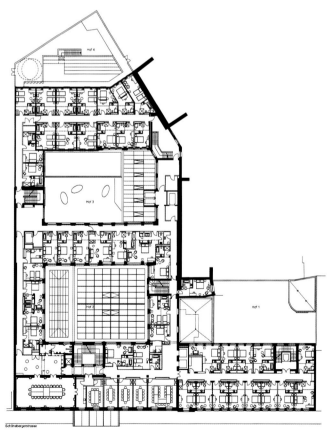

Schönebergerstrasse

Schönebergerstrasse

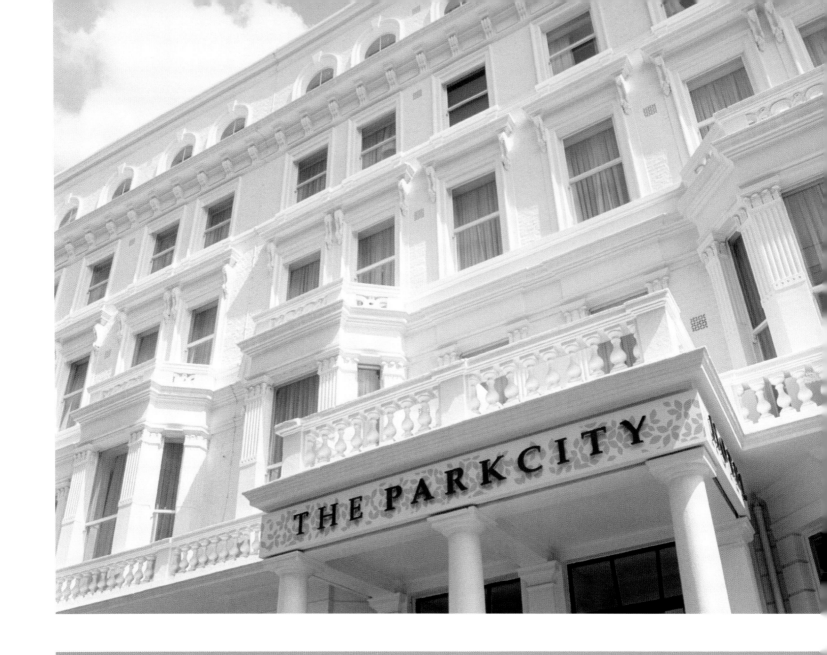

Designer: SHH / Date: 2005 / Location: London, UK / Photographer: Francesca Yorke

Parkcity Hotel

SHH created a new luxury four-star hotel called Parkcity on Lexham Gardens in London's Gloucester Road area, for private client Parkcity Properties Ltd. The brief for the project was to transform an existing rundown two-star, 96-room hotel into a £10m, four-star, 64-room luxury hotel (comprising 62 rooms and two 3-bed apartments).

The hotel was originally formed out of seven Victorian houses, built in the early part of the 19th century. Besides a lot of structural work, SHH created an interior treatment based on an over-riding feel of restrained elegance. SHH created a new, controlled single hotel entrance, a hugely increased lobby area, a new bar to the restaurant's rear (Ruby's), a new Cafeteria /Breakfast Room (The Garden Room) and a dedicated restaurant on the lower-ground area.

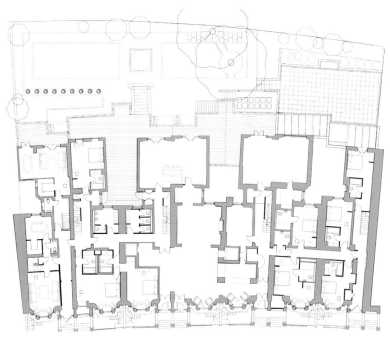

Designer: GRAFT, Lars Krückeberg, Wolfram Putz, Thomas Willemeit / Date: 2004
Location: Berlin, Germany / Photographer: hiepler brunier architekturfotografie & Graft

Q HOTEL

GRAFT laid out a hotel landscape, which changes the classic spatial canon through the topographical folding of the program. The tectonic logic element construction distorts itself and blends into hybrid zones with double functional occupancies. The inclined area is simultaneously a separating wall and usable furniture; the lifted floor is circulation surface or a space, emerging from underneath the skin of the house.

The flow of this "landscape" creates generous connections where otherwise a typical dissection into singular spaces would prevail. The topographical treatment of the design problem maximises programme utilization and creates a continuous flow of form and space. The visitor will find a narrative that departs from conventional perceptual experiences and allows ambiguous readings of the space.

The inhabitant becomes participant on this landscape, changing his interaction with the architecture and the furniture. He walks up the walls in order to sit on top of the celebrating crowd. Or he sinks into the tubs, that offer themselves like hot springs in the ground in the middle of the room.

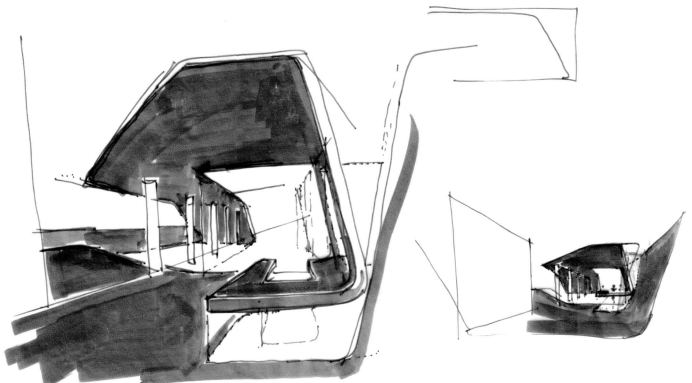

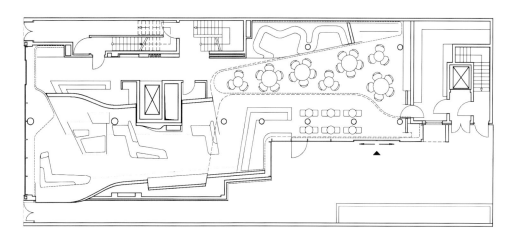

Designer: MKV Design / Location: Zagreb, Croatia

Regent Esplanade

MKV Design totally re-planned all five floors of guestrooms increasing the keys from 173 to 209. They attribute all rooms share supreme comfort and a feeling of "coming home" that is enriched with original paintings from the Esplanade's substantial collection of work by famous Croatian artists.

The guestrooms have very generously sized and beautifully appointed bathrooms.

There is a presidential suite, comprising a sitting/dining room, two bedrooms and bathrooms, a butler's suite, a sauna and a Jacuzzi. In the guestroom corridors, black and white photographs of Orient Express travellers at Zagreb station remind today's guests of the Hotel's early connection with adventure and travel of the movie.

The Regent Esplanade has become a hotel today within the venerable tradition of the great hotels of the world. The aim has been to ensure that even the new elements feel somehow as if they have always been there. This Hotel should not date.

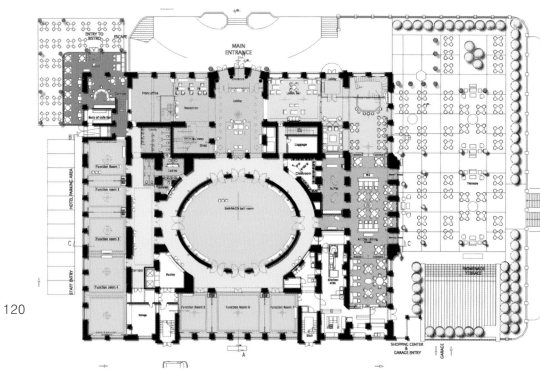

Designer:Bost Berlin / Date: 2006 / Location: Leipzig, Germany
Photographer: The Radisson SAS Leipzig

Radisson SAS Hotel

Radisson SAS Hotel Leipzig was completely renovated. The transformation of the building included three main fields of work: the reduction of rooms for the purpose of extension, the covering of the front with a new glass facade to achieve light drenched rooms and, finally, the renewal of all installations.

A fresh and juvenescent business characteristic of dramatic elements was given to the hotel. The carpet in the lobby in red and beige reminds evokes classic Burlington pattern. The bar affects with dashes of dramatic red, contrasted by bronze and golden tones. Contrary to the corridors, the guestrooms are spacious and brightly lighted due to the glass facade. It is a claim of a modern business hotel.

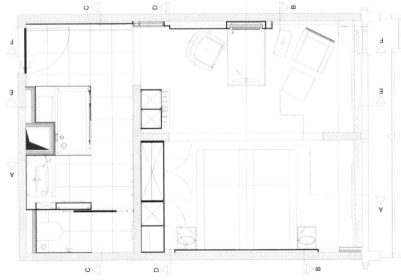

Designer: Lian Maria Bauer Projektdesign / Date: 2003 / Location: Switzerland
Photographer: Christoph Grünig

Rose Castle Risegg

Rose Chateau Risegg is located on a hill of a vineyard. The building is from a distance visible with its characterized small towers on each corner of the building ensemble.

The design starts in the entrance hall and staircase. Nearly 200 pictures and framed photos show the life and experiences in the past. The pictures hightlight the flavour of history and tradition. The closed "Café der Musen" fascinates with clear abstraction design and is an attractive place for communication, active relaxing and refreshing.

A mix of ancient, new and interesting elements and the entireness of the ensemble were created from the bathroom to deeper details like textiles.

Through the "Galleria of heroines" the guests arriving at the upper floors and have the choice of six thematic designed suites. Each of the 3 floors offers a big suite with 83 squave metres and a smaller suite with 67 squave metres. The design of each suite is dedicate to popular women and reflect the character of these women.

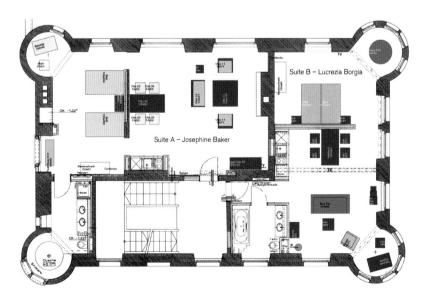

Suite B – Lucrezia Borgia

Suite A – Josephine Baker

139

Designer: DiLeonardo International, Inc. / Date: 2007 / Location: Changsha, China
Photographer: DiLeonardo International, Inc.

Sheraton Hotel

The hotel entry and lobby is an experience of international modern luxury. In working within the expectations of the Sheraton brand we have created a space which will make discerning international travelers feel the excitement of this timeless deign. The overall design direction reinforces the contemporary architecture of the Yunda development combined with comfortable over scaled and dramatic design elements.

The guestroom is the heart of the hotel and here we emphasise the Sheraton Brand while providing a comfortable residential environment for the international travelers. The guests here will feel the tailored sophistication of this environment as an extension of this world class development.

Sheraton Hotel, Changsha is an exciting and timeless experience combining a sense of tailored sophistication with modern luxury and the guests know they are part of the premier project that will set the standard for the entire region.

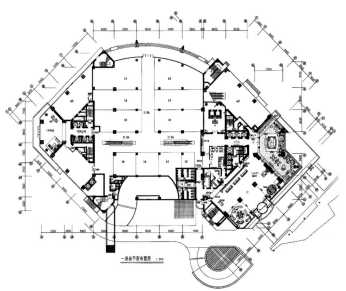

一层总平面布置图 1/200

145

Designer: Lian Maria Bauer Projektdesign / Date: 2003 / Location: Switzerland
Photographer: Christoph Grünig

Seerose Hotel

Designer Lian Maria Bauer designed the entire interior for the hotel and restaurant in colours of four elements: fire, water, earth and air as well as with forms and tangible emotions with an immense number of surprising details.

The subject fire is realized in the basement story for the business-room and the impressing vault of the wine cellar which are all designed in nut tree and equipped with louvre doors on light stone ground. The Subject of water welcomes the guests on the first floor. The fluent grain of Zebrano-wood of the furnishing on the light bamboo floor emphasizes the subject of the element water and gives the necessary warmth for the cooler blue tone and green tones of the walls and textiles. The Subject earth presents itself the visitor in the second story. The arrangement fascinates with a dark Wenge at the ground and is equipped like almost all rooms with a cupboard unit and a basin which form the boundary of the open bath. The severity of the Wenge forms the contrast to the spicy colours of "Safran" and "Cayenne".

The visitor finds in the attic the subject of air. In each room of this floor, a metamorphosis lamp contributes its illusionary light which can create many different light emotions. The walls coloured in airy pastels and textiles help to reflect the spectacle of light.

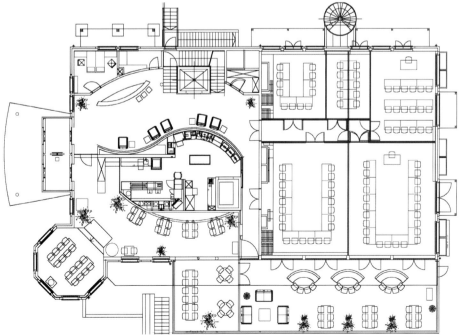

Designer: Matteo Thun and Annette Schafer / Date: 2000 / Location: Hamburg, Germany

Side Hotel

Side Hotel made an effective mix of curved lines and straight lines: an eight-story body in glass inserted into a load bearing structure made of green stone. Once within the hall, the thing that strikes one most is the light – changing hourly and following the seasons.

It is really the five senses upon which we base all design and philosophical speculations. There coexists at Side, thus, meditations on these five themes: the tactile found in the diverse materials and surface finishes; the visual revealed in the natural chiaroscuro of light interacting with colours that sometimes can make them seem faint and sometimes, bright; the sound and smell which characterize each area of the hotel with a particular suffused music and particular subtle fragrance; and ultimately the taste, which one encounters in the area dedicated to the bar and restaurant .

Although each of these areas may have their distinct and particular connotative aspect, they form an architectonic whole. They succeed in integrating themselves into an ensemble through the continual recall of form, material and light.

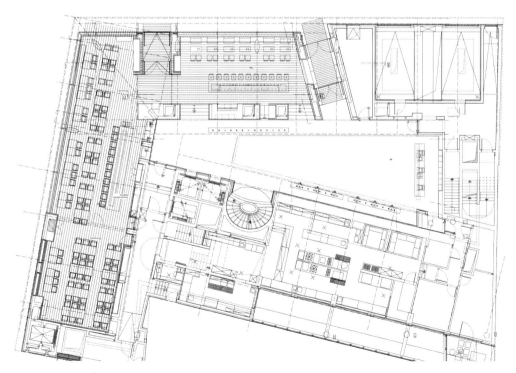

Designer: Stefano Severi / Date: 2003 / Location: Modena, Italy
Photographer: Alberto Ferrero

Touring Hotel

It is a four star hotel that was renovated three years ago through the adoption of a contemporary style. Modern and minimal communal interiors are characterized by sober and discreet elegance, which is coupled with great attention to detail.

The warm light cast by paper lampshades enhances ethnic and colonial objects, bleached oak and matt finish laminates, next to warm earthy and sandy colours and different shades of brown. Woven hemp rugs, large mirrors and floral decorations are the sober features of classic but original interiors. Modern and minimal communal interiors are characterized by sober and discreet elegance, which is coupled with great attention to detail.

The first floor houses the Blue Bar, a cosy place that is open all day long. The bar serves breakfast and lunch during the day, while acting as a meeting place in the evening, serving aperitifs and local food and wine tasting sessions. The hotel has a total of 68 guest rooms that are arranged on the upper levels. They feature different colour schemes: The rooms set in the left wing of the hotel are painted light blue, while the rooms in the right wing are green. Finally the rooms located in the central wing are salmon-coloured.

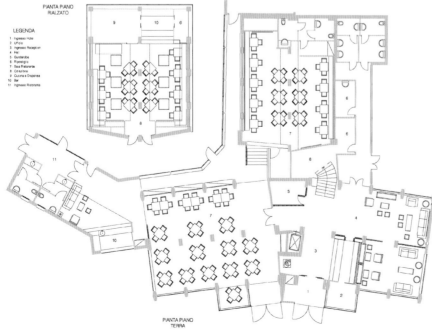

Designer: Bost Berlin – Interieur Design / Date: 2006 / Location: Dresden, Germany
Photographer: Westin Bellevue Hotel

The Westin Bellevue Hotel

Bost Berlin completely renovated the central baroque part of Westin Bellevue Hotel in Dresden, Germany. Modern Art functionalism has been masterly composed with neo-baroque opulence.

The stairway has been modernised by the addition of a glazed lift. They rebuilt one central courtyard to an impressive glass roofed lobby. The old groin vault of the appropriate wine cellar has been jazzed up with rosewood furniture and a marble floor.

They have redesigned 14 luxury suites. Spa is set within the suites, and glazed bathrooms mounts as an integral element into the living area. The relaxing effect is supported by a methane gas fireplace in each suite. Elegant furniture, fine fabrics, Italian granite and illuminated light panels in the ceiling put the finishing touches to the interiors. An innovative air-conditioning system caters for the perfect room climate in the suite

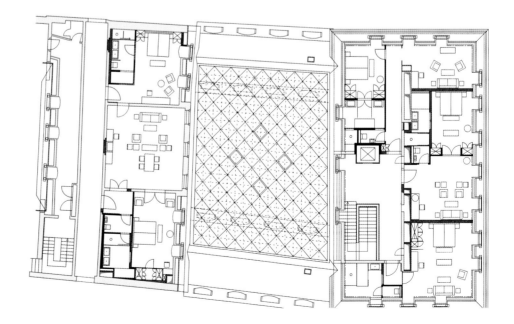

175

Designer: Guido Ciompi / Location: Milano, Italy / Date: 2003
Photographer: Martin Kunz, Roland Bauer, Giulio Oriani

The Gray Hotel

Created by the highly recognized Italian architect and interior designer Guido Ciompi, the Gray offers 21 uniquely designed guest rooms and public spaces. Each space offers a relaxing concept of hospitality. A hot pink swing in the lobby greets guests as a colourful pattern of lights projected on the walls creates the hotel's "Lobby Art".

Adjacent to the Lobby an iron staircase leads up to the intimate Le Noir restaurant, which is marked by brightly coloured stripes of lighting, an innovative black box for lounging and a chandelier dangling with antique silver spoons and forks. This attractive setting will be open for breakfast, lunch and dinner and feature traditional and modern Italian cuisine. Next to the Lobby is the intimate Il Bar featuring a plasma screen reflecting earth and water images that transmit sound.

This innovative style is further exemplified in the 21 guest rooms. With furniture created by Italian artisans, the rooms, all a bit different, are a tasteful blend of the exotic dark striped wenge wood and almost black makassar wood, filmy white curtains, leather furniture and dramatic quilted headboards. African inspired art and bright orange accent pieces contribute to the sophisticated and contemporary design of each room. Some of the specialty guest rooms feature an in suite gym or steam bath, while a number of the bathrooms offer large circular tubs fitted with TV screens on the rims. In the duplex rooms the bed is suspended from the ceiling with steel cables.

Designer: Vincenzo de Cotiis / Date: 2004 / Location: Milano, Italy

The Straf Hotel

The STRAF project arose from the need to turn a new page regarding the currently clichéd concept of a "hotel".

STRAF demonstrates a differentiation between the types of rooms and creates defined spaces which are characterized by materials that are combined according to two main approaches: black slate or cement combined with burnished brass, with mirrored walls giving an overall effect of space.

The personalized design of the rooms demonstrates macro-decorative elements which, according to aesthetic value, create an effect of expansion for the space by using illusionary perspectives, such as wall paneling and palisades that appear to extend into infinity.

This hotel is identified by its alternative to clichés and standardizations. It is a "place of choice" that turns away from production line furnishings. This emphasis is reflected throughout the hotel, from the bathrooms which are fitted with worn mirrors and designer sinks, to the tailor made chairs, sofas and the lighting.

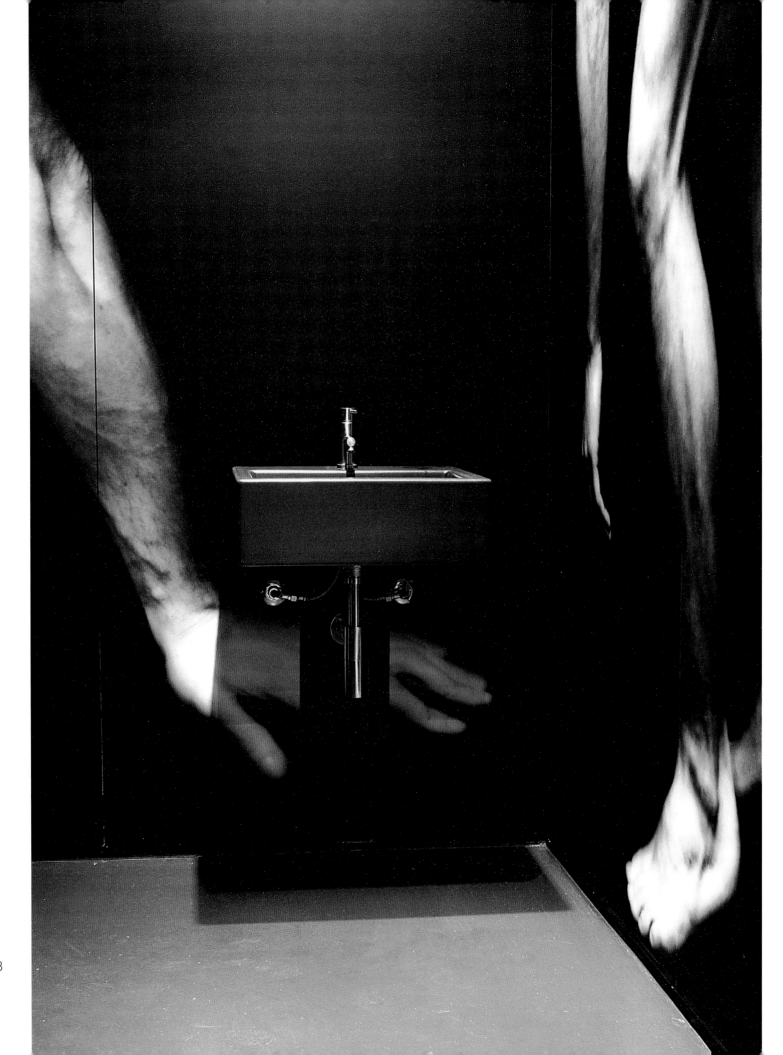

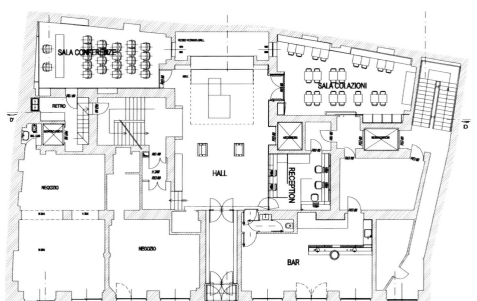

199

Designer: MKV Design / Date: 2005 / Location: Vienna, Austria
The Style Hotel

The Style Hotel, built in the center of Vienna in 2005, is a contemporary interpretation of Vienna's early 1020s Secession Art Nouveau. With the hotel located at the intersection of four streets, it was possible to have all rooms and suites looking outwards. High ceiling and large windows maximize natural light and provide splendid views of the Old Center of Vienna.

The hotel has 600 sq meters of communal premises arranged around a high atrium. Two lifts link the lobby with the upper floors. A large Art Deco chandelier dominates the center of the foyer. Golden ornaments, glass and subtle lighting feature throughout the hotel. Although the individual rooms vary in size they share certain features –modern, colorful furniture, Italian glass in the baths and mirrored TV screens. Rounding out the hotel's perfectly balanced atmosphere are the recurring colours—cream and crimson—and dark wooden, leather and chrome building materials.

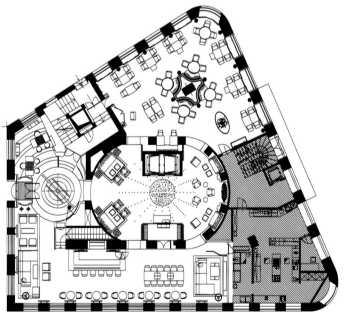

Designer: Concrete Architectural Associates / Date: 2005 / Location: Bremen, Germany
Photography: Jeroen Musch

Überfluss Hotel

The zebrano covered floor and the silver leaf ceiling guide the guests to the bar and the restaurant area located on the Schlachte side.The border of this area is marked by a wooden walkway intersecting the diagonal.Next to it in the heart of this space the bar is located. Here the two lines, diagonal and parallel, shape the furniture. The other part of the bar is finished in chrome steel.

Next to the bar is the lounge. Low black glossy tables form the centre of this area that is dimly lit using both chrome bolster downlights and chrome Kaipo table lights. A three-meter wide "fireplace" in the wall enhances the lounge atmosphere. Black lace curtains in front of the dark grey glass soften up the place to create a nice cosy corner.Generally speaking the room is divided in to two areas, the bathroom, bed and other 'fixed' elements are part of a black rectangle 'inserted' in the room.

The suite is roughly divided into three areas. Firstly the area, at the entrance, connects the corridor to the room. Here the striped carpet covers the floor. There is a large black glossy table with two glass-door fridges underneath.Between the Jacuzzi and the sitting area in the room, a dark grey glass pane stops the water splashing into the room and together with the lightcurtain it obscures the view a little to make it more intimate.

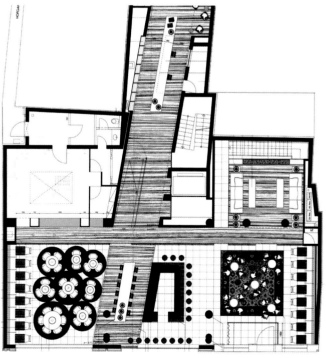

Designer: Jordi Cuenca, Jordi Clos, Carles Bassó, Mariano Martitegui / Date: 2004
Location: Madrid, Spain

Urban Hotel

HOTEL URBAN is divided into an incredible terrace soaring over the Madrid skyline, and a Glass bar and a Europa decoration that are the current culinary hotspots. At Urban, there are neither fads nor manners. There is energy and inner light that provoke a tense beauty. Anything can happen at Urban, and everything can belong to everyone, from the rooftop terrace to the meeting rooms.

This building's design was based on the objective of creating a New Classical Order, aimed at blending with the historical buildings and monuments that make up this urban landscape. From the intimate and transparent swimming pool tucked away on one side, to the most fashionable sinuous corner in Madrid, all types of materials coexist at Urban.So do all types of energies, all types of concepts. There is Alabaster, marble, Wengé wood parquetry, ebony, limestone, tropical teak wood panels, steel, glass, gold-tiled panels, Déco-style wood, Chinese lacquer ware, leather canopies, green Guatemala and white Thassos marble slabs. The small terrace towards the back, with totems from Papua New Guinea, transports the guests to another world.

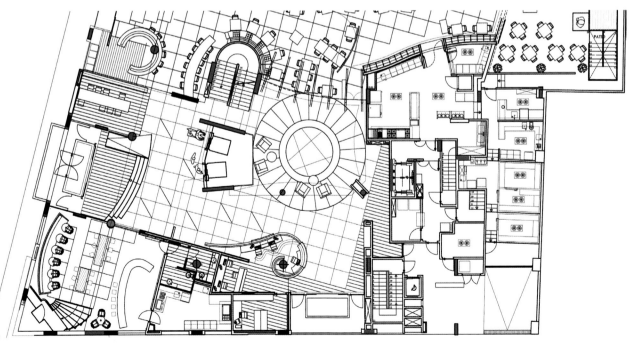

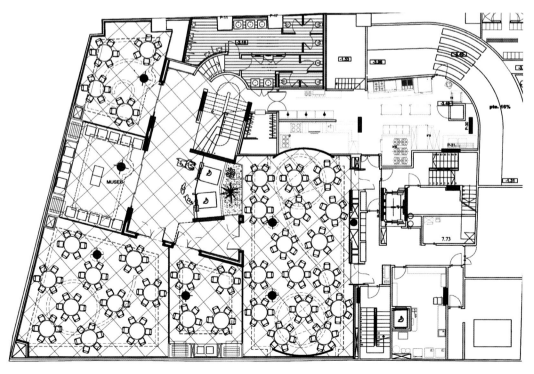

Designer: Carl Ross Design, Inc. / Date: 2003 / Location: Colorado, USA
Photographer: David O. Marlow, Robert Miller

Valdoro Mountain Lodge

This new-construction is located in the Rocky Mountains of Breckenridge, Colorado. The interior design is built around creating a strong, sophisticated connection to the high-country heritage of the local area using a palette of natural, local materials and finishes blended with the high quality services and amenities which guests have come to expect in the upscale market.

Each of the guest villas features granite countertops, upgraded stainless steel appliances, and custom stained cherry cabinetry with glass doors and stained hardwood millwork throughout. Living rooms feature a dry-stack stone fireplace using local indigenous stone and a monolithic sandstone slab hearth and mantle. The bedrooms feature a duvet and blanket combination with accent fabric bolster and pillow shams with a custom, hand-made found-object wood sculpture over each bed.

The furniture within each suite is designed to reflect the subtle references to the Rocky Mountains via the patterns, colors, textures and prints. Each villa bathroom is four-fixture and features full-height stone-wrapped showers and Jacuzzi spa tubs, granite slab counters, cherry wood vanities and an inset-patterned stone floor. The scenery here is full of local taste.

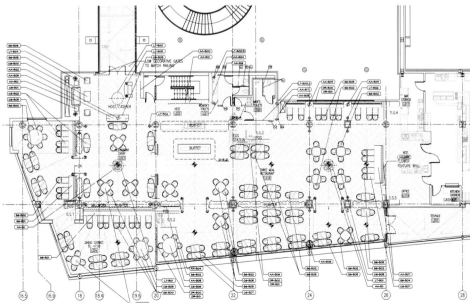

Designer: Matteo Thun / Date: 2005 / Location: Milano, Italy
Vigilius Mountain Resort

Starting with the extension to the existing hotel structure; the new building is an interpretation of traditional, local construction in wood in an absolutely innovative way.

The main part of the building extends itself in length in the North–South direction and is composed of three floors,including the basement: a volume which is lying on the ground and which becomes, with its profile, an integral part of the landscape.

The integration of the building into its natural surroundings is underlined also by the use of a "green roof" (plants, garden, water) which can be used by guests. A further, new part of the construction is the restaurant "Ida", which replaces the old structure in position and volume, but this re-interpretation is completely integrated with the new building.

The longitudinal form of the building allows for a heightened theatrical experience of nature. The private spaces: bedrooms, alternate with public spaces: the swimming pool, the treatment spaces and the large terraces in a dynamic way.

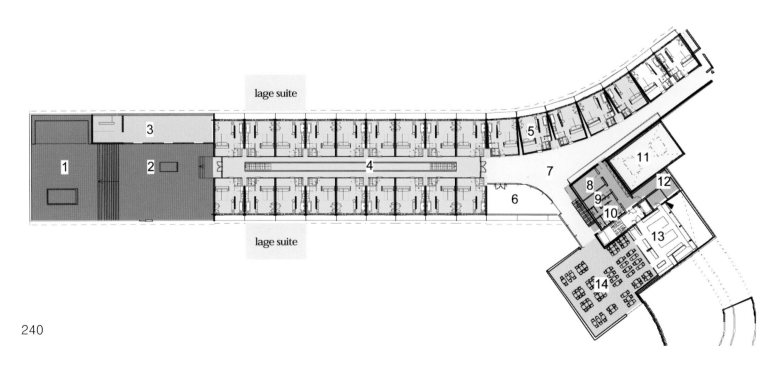

lage suite

lage suite

1

2

3

4

5

6

7

8

9

10

11

12

13

14

Designer: Heller Manus Architects, Inc. / Date: 2005 / Location: San Francisco, USA
Photographer: Heller Manus Architects, Jeffrey Newbury and Cesar Rubio

Vitale Hotel

Hotel Vitale is consciously designed to appeal to post-hip guests aged from 35 to 55 who have outgrown the hip boutique hotel and are not ready for the formality of an ultra-expensive 5 star brand. Such customers are active adventurous and creative, looking for a nurturing urban hotel experience—they are more interested in spa than a bar. With its emphasis on natural building materials and sumptuous soothing modern interior design, Hotel Vitale not only lives up to its tag line of luxurious and natural, but also includes the key qualities—Modern, Urbane, Revitalizing, Fresh, and Nurturing, which have steered the development of every aspect of the hotel and underpin the extraordinary swift success of this project.

Occupancy rates have exceeded expectations, for the guests have responded so enthusiastically to this project that holds their dearest values to heart. The guests range from business men to leisure travelers who expressed their feeling by saying "We not only left our hearts in san Francisco, but ourselves at Hotel Vitale". The hotel also provides a complimentary long term luggage storage service and they can find them in their rooms until next visit.

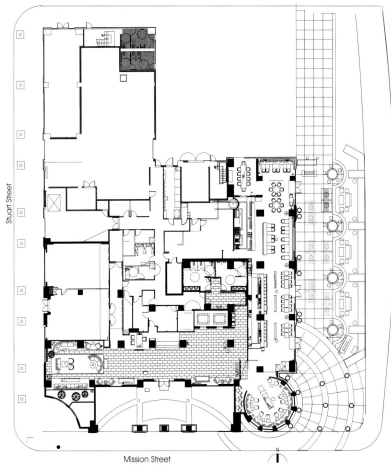

Stuart Street

Mission Street

Designer: Tassilo Bost / Date: 2006 / Location: Berlin, Germany
Photographer: Martin Karras

Westin Grand Hotel

Tassilo Bost designed the Schinkel Suite, which is part of the Presidential Suite at Westin Grand Hotel Berlin. The new optics expresses the spirit of classicism by translating the language of shapes and colours into a contemporary, purified understanding. The forms are clear and geometric. The spatial organization was clarified, and the former colouring was changed to elegant monochrome white, supported by high value materials of Teak wood, white Greek marble and fine fabrics.

The designers used ornaments selectively for special purposes. As an excerpt of classicism, chrome plated fittings decorate the white coated furniture: chrome lines on cabinet doors, chrome table-legs and mirrors with chrome frames. A hint of "royalty" is also provided by shiny organza curtains and glace coloured cushions with metallic applications.

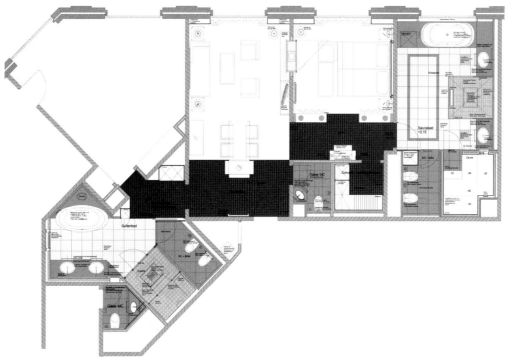

Designer: Mohen Design International / Date: 2004 / Location: Shanghai, China
Photographer: Shangqin Mo
Xiangshan Hotel

Occupying the 15th floor of a high-rise condo in the very center of Shanghai, the apartment overlooks the downtown skyline. Its planning is precise and simple, however, interpreted in a very moderate way. A rusted, visually rough entry wall of metal leads the eyes peeking into the apartment and serves as a functional built-in storage as well.

Private space is separated from public by an endless bamboo focal point, uplift by floor lamps, and illusioned by semi-transparent front glass. Primary finish materials include rough grayish Chinese granite, stainless steel, rusted metal and oak veneer. A highly articulated wheel assembles the huge metal-hinged door of the master bedroom, and further emphasized by the arc symbol on the wood floor, assuming great prominence. The dinning table is a floating plane of steel extruding to a circular water vase at the end where it supports for a hidden metal structure. In a city in which interior tends to be messy and westernized, this apartment stands out with its finely honed Shanghai elegance.

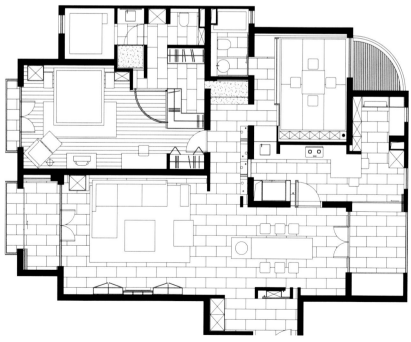

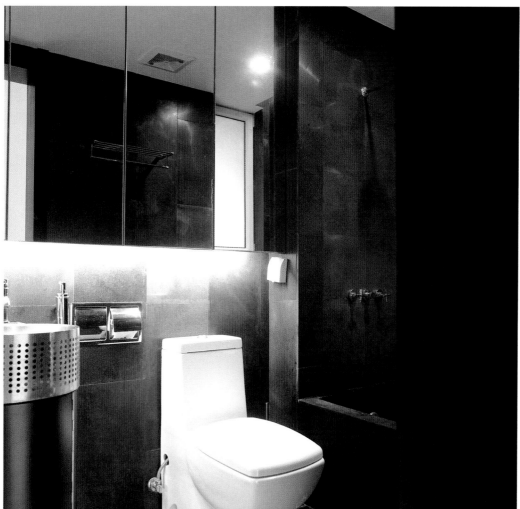

Designer: Precious McBane / Date: 2004 / Location: London, UK

Zetter Hotel

Precious McBane created an environment that both locals and visitors alike would visit, whether to meet, eat or simply sleep; It is like a modern urban inn. Chetwood Architects sensitively converted the old Zetter pools warehouse and Precious McBane were excited to be given a loose reign on the design of the entire interior.

It was an opportunity to use pattern and colour to explore a more decorative direction in hotel design. With each bedroom decorated individually Precious McBane managed to create a domestic feel within the restored warehouse, from the hand embroidered blankets to the Penguin Classics by the bed. By contrasting floral patterns with iconic mid-century design pieces, Precious McBane created a distinctive and sophisticated environment in its own idiosyncratic style.

Architekt Rainer Seiferth

Hagelberger Str. 18
D-10965 Berlin
r.seiferth@arcor.de
Tel : 0049-(0)30-692 42 42
Fax: 0049-(0)30-691 23 56
www.rainerseiferth.com

Zum Lebenslauf: geboren am 8.2.1955 in Landshut/Niederbayern studierte in Berlin an der HDKseit 1986 Freischaffender Architekt in Berlin.Individualbüro für alle Leistungsphasen des Planens und Bauens.Schwerpunkt: Reanimierung vernachlässigter Wohn- und Gewerbehöfe .Weitere Bauten: Auguststr. 35, 36, 91, Kalkscheune u.a. in Berliner InnenbezirkenIn Arbeit: Gewerbehof Brunnenstr.10, Dachaufbau Kalkscheune und Zelt-Segel im Hof

bost berlin – Interieur Design . Architecture

Danckelmannstrasse 9 D-14059 BERLIN (Germany)
Tel : +49 (0) 30 30 12 11 -14
Fax: +49 (0) 30 30 12 11 -17
www.bost-interieurdesign.de
info@bost-interieurdesign.de

The team at Bost Berlin specialises in interior architecture and design of top-of-the-range hotels. The architects and designers led by Tassilo Bost realise modernistic concepts of interior design for groups such as Arabella Sheraton, The Westin, Le Méridien and Kempinski. The Berlin agency's international success is founded on an interdisciplinary approach combining architecture, interior and product design. The team's expressive design ideas provide a sustainable contribution to the future conception of the hotel as a living and working environment. The achievements of Bost Berlin were honoured most recently at the European Hotel Design Awards in London where they won in the category Best Guestroom Design.

Concrete Architectural Associates.

Rozengracht 133 III / 1016 LV Amsterdam / The Netherlands
Tel : 020. 5200200
Fax: 020. 5200201
www.concreteamsterdam.nl
Info@concreteamsterdam.nl

Concrete architectural associates is founded in 1997 by Rob Wagemans, Gilian Schrofer and Erik van Dillen. They met each other by a not realized project, a head office in Amsterdam for Cirque du soleil.Rob Wagemans, (present director of Concrete Architectural Associates)Born in Eindhoven on 13th of February 1973,History of education: HTS university of construction in Utrecht, academy of architecture in Amsterdam. Erik van Dillen (at this moment he is only creative involved by concrete)
Born in de Bilt on 27th of April 1960, History of education: interior architect, Rietveld academy, catering industry skills in the kitchen, painting restorer.Gilian Schrofer left concrete in 2004 to start his own company.Concrete Reinforced is founded in 2006 by Rob Wagemans and Erikjan Vermeulen. They are friends and were colleges in school. Reinforced is responsible for architecture and urban landscaping and enriches concrete with its disciplines.Erikjan Vermeulen (present director of Concrete Reinforced)Born in Texel on the 2nd of april 1973.History of education: HTS university of construction in Utrecht, academy of architecture in Amsterdam. Worked for different architects to start his own company in 2003.

Carl Ross Design

W115 Main Street
El Segundo, CA 90245
Tel : 310-333-1982
Fax: 310-333-1982
www.carlrossdesign.com
carlr@carlrossdesign.com

Carl Ross Design, Inc. offers premium interior design services for the domestic and international 4- to 5-star hotel and resort markets, from master planning through installation. Our team's qualifications are the result of over 20 years' commitment to hospitality design, including full-service destination resorts, business hotels, spas, conference facilities, luxury boutique hotels, timeshare, and restaurants. Our design objective is to create authentic design which responds to a project's locale, market, and clientele. It's our belief that successful, distinctive projects incorporate an artful balance of time, budget, and quality with the mutual respect, chemistry, and teamwork of the project team members.

DiLeonardo International, Inc.

2350 Post Rd., Suite 1
Warwick, RI 02886
Tel : (401) 732-2900
Fax: (401) 732-5315

The architectural interior design firm of DiLeonardo International is recognized worldwide for achievements and innovations in the hospitality industry. Headquartered in the US of America, the firm manages offices throughout the world to assure the most culturally-sensitive designs and the most effective administration of its projects.
Cultural sensitivity is more than respect. It is the creation of a strong sense of place. It is the bridge that connects travelers to the special character and experience of their destination. With each assignment, DiLeonardo's specialized experience, integrity and collaborative skills combine to expand the definition of hospitality to the greater benefit and satisfaction of guests, owners and operators, alike.
The firm's portfolio of completed projects is a visionary collection of more than 1000 resorts, hotels, casinos, conference centers and restaurants located around the globe. Under the leadership of its founder, Robert DiLeonardo, PhD, the forward-thinking, creative concepts of the firm's designers and architects have earned DiLeonardo International the industry's most prestigious awards. The beauty and distinctive character of each DiLeonardo design is always in seamless balance with the client's objectives, assuring both the aesthetic and financial success of each project.

GRAFT

Gesellschaft von Architekten mbH
Borsigstrasse 33 10115 Berlin Deutschland
Tel: 030 / 2404 79-85 oder -86
www.graftlab.com

In January 1998 the GRAFT has been created in Los Angeles as a label for architecture, art, music and the "pursuit of happiness". Lars Kruckeberg, Wolfram Putz and Thomas Willemeit are the partners of GRAFT that today employs about 20 architects and artists in the US, Europe and in Asia. GRAFT has offices in Los Angeles and Berlin. A third office is planned to open in Beijing, China January 2005.

Heller Manus Architects

221 MAIN STREET, SUITE 940
SAN FRANCISCO, CA94105-1923
Tel : 415-247-1100
INFO@HELLERMANUS.COM
WWW.HELLERMANUS.COM

Heller Manus Architects has spent more than 20 years in developing a diversified, client oriented firm. We have always avoided a singular signature approach. Instead, we focus on finding the H ideal design solution for each commission. The firm's portfolio of projects has been expanding since 1984. Projects range from master plans to in-fill buildings, large and small-scale retail designs to high-rise residential and office towers, transit shelters to City Halls, and Beaux-Arts landmark renovations to streamlined transportation facilities, all share a common characteristic: high-quality, cost-effective design, sensitive to the projects users' function, site, and civic significance. In addition to numerous commissions in the San Francisco Bay Area, the firm has completed prominent buildings throughout the United States, many of which have been honored with national awards for their design quality and seamless contextuality. Longstanding client relationships, including nationally prominent organizations and repeat business testify to the success of Heller Manus' unique personal approach.

Hotel Urban

C/ València, 284 08007 Barcelona, Spain
Tel : +34 93 366 88 00
Fax: +34 93 366 88 11
www.derbyhotels.com

With meticulous attention to the details, in the rooms and suites at the Urban one can enjoy the harmony of materials that, in combination with lighting carefully designed for every space and good soundproofing, ensure maximum comfort throughout the hotel.
All 96 rooms feature different pieces from Asian cultures belonging to the hotel's ancient art collection. All the rooms are equipped with individually-controlled heating and air conditioning units, a two-line telephone, a safe for laptop computers, parquet flooring, music system, hair dryer, wireless Internet access, DVD player, flat-screen LCD, satellite TV channels, Canal Plus and interactive digital TV. Amongst its other amenities, the hotel also boasts 24-hour room service and an array of premium gastronomic and leisure options with its three restaurants and bars: Europa Decó, Glass Bar and La Terraza del Urban. To relax, the best bets are the swimming pool with its own sunroom, and the archaeological museum with the private collection of the Clos Archaeological Foundation.
The Hotel Urban is located in the Madrid of the Austrias just a few minutes' walk from the triangle of museums made up of the Prado, the Thyssen-Bornemisza and the Reina Sofía. Other points of interest just a stone's throw away are the congress house, the Retiro Park and the Puerta del Sol.

JOI Design

JOI-Design Innenarchitekten GmbH
Medienpark [k]ampnagel
Barmbeker Strape 6a
D- 22303 Hamburg
Germany
Tel : + 49 / (0) 40 / 68 94 21 – 50
Fax: + 49 / (0) 40 / 68 94 21 – 30
www.JOI-Design.com
info@JOI-Design.com

Interior design is an essential success metric in hotel business, restaurant and the wellness trade. Design must not be interchangeable but should contribute to a project's placement and be considered as unique. We can prove that regarding these aspects it doesn't concern merely empty talk. Our team's aim is to please the investor, the operating company and above all the guest, to make them happy. In this connection, we don't strive for self-realisation but consider a good design as an instrument for a conjoint success. Our experience supports this task: Some of our staffers can possess more than 20 years of experience regarding international hotel design. They are being supported by young creatives that contribute fresh ideas to our projects. With this know-how, we ensure a functional processing and the implementation of technical and operational demands which guarantee an economical operation. Regarding our international projects, we don't allow the classical service portrait of interior designers and architects to set us limits. Brand appearances are part of our range of activities as well as project studies or complete corporate identity conceptions. And although we are working with most up to date equipment, the creative, brief draft hasn't fallen into oblivion. Whatever we do, we attach great importance to a close communication with our clients. Solutions are being developed together, since new conceptions and creative ideas always emerge individually reaching a consensus. But see for yourself!

Jestico + Whiles

1 Cobourg Street, London NW1 2HP
Tel : +44 (0) 20 7380 0382
Fax: +44 (0) 20 7380 0511
www.jesticowhiles.com

Jestico + Whiles is a leading British architectural practice based in London and Prague with an international reputation for quality of design and technical innovation.
Jestico + Whiles was established in 1977 and has carried out projects throughout Europe and Asia . The practice is committed to producing intelligent, practical solutions with clear architectural qualities.
As award-winning architects with a strongly commercial background our expertise lies in realising the maximum potential for clients, whilst also securing the broadest architectural and environmental benefits from each project.

Kleihues + Kleihues

Gesellschaft von Architekten mbH
Helmholtzstr. 42
D-10587 Berlin
Tel : +49 30 39 97 79-0
Fax: +49 30 39 97 79-77
www.kleihues.com
berlin@kleihues.com

A responsible approach to designing high quality inhabitable space is the underlying philosophy of this office. As a result, the buildings by Kleihues + Kleihues distinguish themselves through a timeless modern design which respects the context of the location. The buildings are functional and enduring – characteristics that Kleihues + Kleihues understand to be the basic requirements for an economical and ecological approach towards working with existing resources. Out of this originates the strong emphasis on the detailing, the selection of materials and the quality of the craftsmanship in the execution.

Lian Maria Bauer

Seestrasse 18
CH-8800 Thalwil / Zürich
Tel : +41-44-772 37 83
Fax: +41-44-772 37 82
www.lian-maria-bauer.com
mail@lian-maria-bauer.com

Lian Maria Bauer Projektdesign creates planes and realizes impressive interior design projects for hotels, restaurants and shops. We define and organize complete and complex projects from small cafes, to ambient restaurants and multi use hotels. We are specialized in approved managing projects from ground and infrastructure planning over creative, temporary design, to complete turn key finishing. Our base is Zurich, Switzerland, but we operate throughout everywhere. A well motivated crew is helping getting projects realized from base architectural planning, over handcraft man ship, to artist work and financial control. We love tore work out the best ideas our clients can get – with cost related thinking and free inspired minds.

MKV Design Ltd

229 – 231 High Holborn
London
WC1V 7DA
Tel : +44 20 7242 2466
Fax: +44 20 7242 2488
www.mkvdesign.com

MKV Design Ltd is an Interior Architectural Design Company specialising in the hospitality sector.Excellence in design achieved through attention to minimum detail and cultural sensitivities is our trademark.Our aim is to provide our clients with the best possible service by understanding their goals and tailoring the product according to the individual project. In the last decade the principal and associated consultants have gained remarkable experience by working closely with various hotel operators, developers and architects in a wide variety of local and international projects.It is our international background that enables us to source materials and ideas world wide and to be up to date with the latest products and designs.We always ensure to produce creative designs within the appropriate budgets, specifications and deadlines.However, most of all, it is our understanding of the business process and the market that allows us to approach the Design in a comprehensive yet unique way in order to help our clients create successful businesses.

MOHEN DESIGN INTERNATIONAL

台湾408台中市南屯区公益路2段51号3楼B2
Tel :+886-932579601
Fax:+886-4-23751995
上海市乌鲁木齐南路396弄18号 200031
Tel:+86-21-64370910/64374175/64374462
Fax:+86-21-64317125
www.mohen-design.com
mohen@mohen-design.com

MOHEN DESIGN INTERNATIONAL is an award-winning company creating schemes for residential, contract, office and hospitality design in Shanghai, Chongqing, Tokyo and Taiwan. The practice was initially set up by Mr. Hank M. Chao as a platform for cross-disciplinary collaborations. MOHEN DESIGN INTERNATIONAL projects range from public buildings to individual interiors for private clients. The practice has particular experience in the leisure and hospitality industry,developers, focusing on the design of contemporary bars, clubs and restaurants, hotels and private villas. Using a unique language of color,light and geometry, our interiorsare sensuous and eventful. Space is carefully choreographed into stylish environments. Each design is treated individually and developed with the help of specialist consultants. Traditional architectural services are complemented with concept and brand development. Established contacts to graphic designers, photographers, media consultants, individual artists offer extended interdisciplinary support. Each project regardless of its size is treated with equal passion and attention to detail. 3-d visualizations allow an immediate insight into an evolving project and form the basis for successful dialogue.

matteo thun

via appiani 9
I-20121 milano
Tel : +39-02-655691-1
Fax: +39-02-6570646
www.matteothun.com
info@matteothun.com

DESIGN INTERNATIONAL projects range from public buildings to individual interiors for private clients. The practice has particular experience in the leisure and hospitality industry,developers, focusing on the design of contemporary bars, clubs and restaurants, hotels and private villas. Using a unique language of color,light and geometry,our interiorsare sensuous and eventful. Space is carefully choreographed into stylish environments. Each design is treated individually and developed with the help of specialist consultants. Traditional architectural services are complemented with concept and brand development. Established contacts to graphic designers, photographers, media consultants, individual artists offer extended interdisciplinary support.We understand the making of architecture as a multi-layered and collaborative process. Close contact to the client is important to develop optimized design solutions. Each project regardless of its size is treated with equal passion and attention to detail. 3-d visualizations allow an immediate insight into an evolving project and form the basis for successful dialogue. Wehave diversified practice that focuses on clients wishing to pursue innovative design strategies. The crew are committed to high quality design and have years of experience controlling their craftsmanship skill and design budget.

Precious McBane

Precious McBane
49–51 Central Street
London
EC1V 8AB
Tel: 0207 253 1510

mail @ preciousmcbane.com

Precious McBane has been established for 10 years. We specialise in thoughtful and imaginative design for interiors and have a passion for exciting product and furniture design. We are a small team with big ideas and frequently collaborate with a range of creatives to satisfy individual briefs. We offer a wide range of services including all aspects of interior design for commercial and private clients, bespoke furniture design, styling and colour consultancy. We approach every project individually and with a creativity that is uniquely Precious McBane. Our Team: Meriel Scott, Sophia Wimpenny and Ali McCulloch. Our Motto: Design, disrupt and delight.

Our Clients: Habitat UK, Nike, Virgin Radio, Vauxhall, Laurent Perrier, British Council, The Zetter Restaurant and Rooms, Bloomburg, Raymond's Revue Bar, Moro, Lux Cinema, Disney, Victoria's Secret, The Mix Colour Consultancy Paul Smith, Prince, Alison Goldfrapp .

Pia M. Schmid

....
....
Architektur und Designbüro
Augustinergasse 25

CH-8001 Zürich

Tel : +41 44 221 08 48
Fax: +41 44 221 08 49
www.piaschmid.ch
info@piaschmid.ch

Before her architecture education Pia Schmid studied at the film-school in Berlin. In 1980 she founded her own architecture firm with a main focus on the hotel sector, gastronomy, wellness as well as public building in Switzerland and abroad. Her work is always a composition that creates a synthesis of a precise analysis and the creative space that develops out of it. Her latest project is a hotel-boat on the river nile

Studio Ciompi

....
....
Via Gino Capponi 44
50121 Firenze
Italy
Tel : 0039055580575
Fax: 0039055577828
www.studiociompi.it

SHH

....
....
1 Vencourt Place
Ravenscourt Park
Hammersmith
London
W6 9NU
Tel: + 44 (0)20 8600 4171
www.shh.co.uk

SHH is an architects' practice and design consultancy, formed by partners David Spence, Graham Harris and Neil Hogan in 1991. The company specialises in workplace design, leisure, retail and residential projects. Clients include Angels the Costumiers, Harvey Nichols, Wales & West, MCCC, ATOC, LA Fitness, Sheraton Hotels, Shaw Park Plaza Hotels, London Zoo, Chelverton, Regalian, The Athenaeum Hotel and the William Pears Group.

STEFANO ARCH. SEVERI

....
....
41012 carpi (mo) ITAL
via rodolfo pio 11
Tel : +39059684812
Fax: +39059684824
www.stefanoseveri.com
info@stefanoseveri.com

The architetect born in 1964 in Carpi (Modena) and take a degree in "Università degli Studi di Firenze" in 1992. In 1994 found the architecture's studio qualified in architecture, design and interior design. Is interested about projetcts of houses, shops, hotels, beauty-centres, bars- restaurants and offices.

Studio di Architettura Fabiola Zeka Lorenzi

....
....
Address: Via Euganea, 53 - 35141 - Padova - Italia
Tel : +39 049 8712992
Fax: +39 049 8712992

www.arketgroup.it
postmaster@arketgroup.it

After a working experience in the field of fashion in the 1980s, she obtained in 1995 a Master's degree in Architecture in the University IUAV of Venice, with a thesis on the restoration and heritage conservation. In the same year she opened a studio in Padua, where she lives. She cooperates with the Office for the Protection of Architectural Heritages in Venice, works on house restoration and, in the last few years, besides many houses, she has designed hotels, restaurants, bars and gyms.

TIHANY DESIGN

....
....
135 West 27th Street, 9th Floor.New York, NY 10001
Tel: 12123665544
www.tihanydesign.com

Tihany Design is a multidisciplinary design atelier with expertise in a broad range of projects with concentration on hospitality design. Founded in 1978, by architect and designer Adam D. Tihany, the firm dedicates itself to custom-tailoring its luxury restaurants and hotels to reflect each client's singular vision and unique brand of hospitality. Known for successfully integrating bold, contemporary designs in landmark spaces, Tihany Design's aesthetic is an unexpected integration of harmony, design and architecture. Fueled by the international background of the firm's principal and itsmulticultural staff, Tihany Design projects — located in several of the world's most cosmopolitan cities and exclusive resorts — are characterized by their strong sense of place. Celebrating the unique tapestry of each particular locale, each project has its own identity and authenticity.

Tilla Theus und Partner AG

....
....
Dipl. Arch. ETH/BSA/SIA
Bionstrasse 18, 8006 Zürich
Tel : +41 44 368 10 10
Fax: +41 44 386 10 20
www.tillatheus.ch
info@tillatheus.ch

Architecture into greatest details is the philosophy and competence of Tilla Theus.
The Ability, Experience and the Love for the job are important facts of her work.
Her Architecture means Precision, Succinctness, Perfection and Charisma.
Tilla Theus is specializing in the design and construction in a demanding urban environment and of protected historical monuments.

Vincenzo de Cotiis

....
....
Studio Next
Immagine e Comunicazione
Via Federico Confalonieri 36
20124 Milano
Tel : 0039 02 6887400
Fax: 0039 02 6684041
www.studionext.it
viviana.coppola@studionext.it

After completing his studies at the Istituto d'Arte, Vincenzo de Cotiis, born in Mantua, graduated in Architecture from the Milan Polytechnic.
The interest in what were to become the trademarks of De Cotiis' work as an architect and interior and fashion designer was already apparent from his early designs: the extremely flexible materials, the recovery of vintage pieces and textiles, given a new lease of life with unusual combinations and colours that blended into the material.